PIANO • VOCAL • GUITAR

The Essential NEIL DIAMOND

ISBN 0-634-05436-8

7777 W. BLUEMOUND RD. P.O. BOX 13819 MILWAUKEE, WI 53213

Visit Hal Leonard Online at
www.halleonard.com

Art Direction (adapted from the matching Columbia CD): Mary Maurer
Design: Mary Maurer, Michael Lau-Robles
Photography: George Hurrell (front cover), Neal Preston (page 4 and back cover)

© 2003 Neil Diamond

CONTENTS

SOLITARY MAN

Words and Music by
NEIL DIAMOND

CHERRY, CHERRY

Words and Music by
NEIL DIAMOND

Ba - by loves me, yes, yes, she does.
Y'ain't got no right, no, no, you don't,

Ah, the girl's out - a - sight, yeah.
ah, to be so ex - cit - ing.

Says she loves me, yes, yes, she does.
Won't need bright lights, no, no, we won't.

To Coda ⊕

Tell your ma - ma, girl, __ I can't stay long.
No, we won't __ tell a soul __ where we gone to.

We got things __ we got __ to catch
Girl, we got we do __ what - ev - er we

up on. Ah, you know, __
want to. Ah, I love __

I GOT THE FEELIN'
(Oh No, No)

Words and Music by
NEIL DIAMOND

Slowly, with feeling

Oh no, no,___ no, no,___
Oh no, no,___ no, no,___

___ ba - by, some - thing's wrong.___
___ you don't smile the same.___

Oh no, no,___ no, no,___ that old time fire is gone.___
Oh no, no,___ no, no,___ like you been hid - in' pain.___

It's not so much the things you say, love.
I love you so much I could taste it,

It's what you don't say I'm a - fraid of. }
but girl, your eyes tell me it's wast - ed. }

I got the feel - in' I'm hear - in' good - bye. __

Don't have to say __ it; it's there in your eyes. __ Oh

KENTUCKY WOMAN

Words and Music by
NEIL DIAMOND

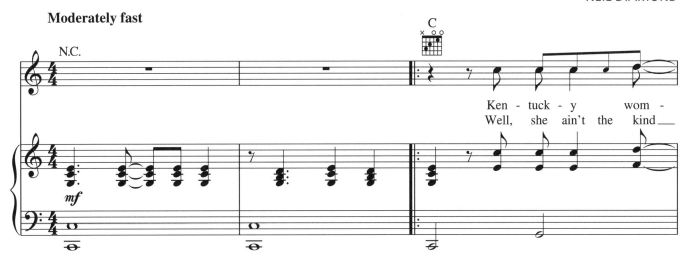

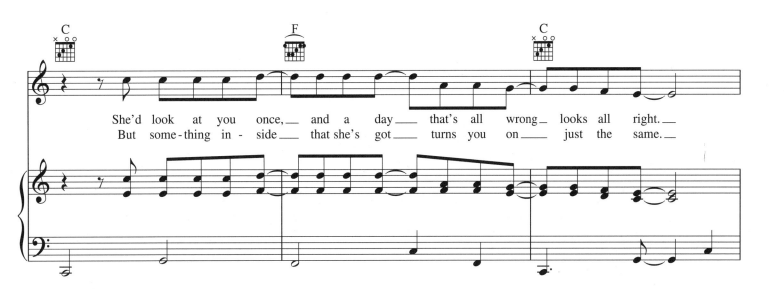

GIRL, YOU'LL BE A WOMAN SOON

Words and Music by
NEIL DIAMOND

YOU GOT TO ME

Words and Music by
NEIL DIAMOND

RED, RED WINE

Words and Music by
NEIL DIAMOND

Slow Country beat

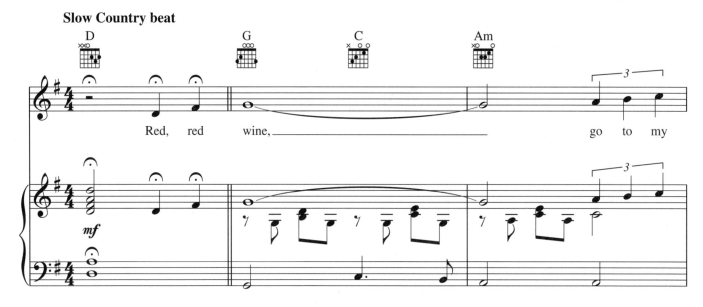

Red, red wine, _____ go to my

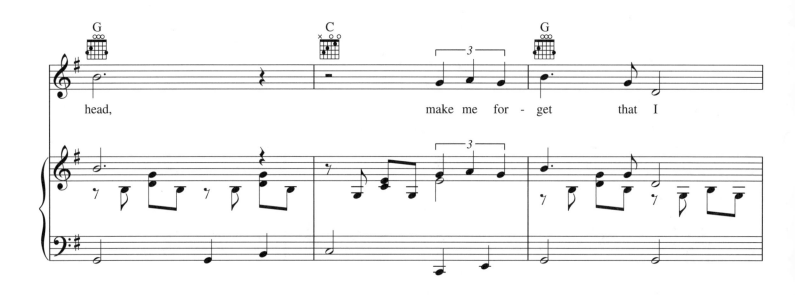

head, make me for-get that I

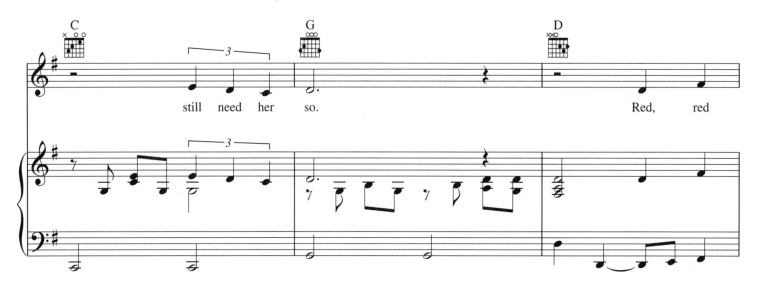

still need her so. Red, red

THANK THE LORD FOR THE NIGHT TIME

Words and Music by
NEIL DIAMOND

I'M A BELIEVER

Words and Music by
NEIL DIAMOND

SWEET CAROLINE

Words and Music by
NEIL DIAMOND

Moderately, very steady

Where it be-gan,____

I can't be-gin to know-in', but then I

SONG SUNG BLUE

Words and Music by
NEIL DIAMOND

blue (blue) weep - in' like a wil - low.

Song (Song) sung (sung) blue (blue) sleep - in' on my pil - low.

Fun - ny thing, ____ but you can sing ____

____ it with a cry in your voice ____

and be - fore you know it start to feel - in' good. _____ You sim - ply got no choice. ____

Fun - ny thing, _____ but you can sing _____ it with a

cry in your voice _____ and be - fore you know it start to feel - in' good. _____

D.S. al Coda

_____ You sim - ply got no choice. _____

CODA

HOLLY HOLY

Words and Music by
NEIL DIAMOND

56

I AM...I SAID

Words and Music by
NEIL DIAMOND

go.

And I'm not a man who likes to swear, but I've nev-er cared for the sound of be-in' a-lone.

"I am," I

CRACKLIN' ROSIE

Words and Music by
NEIL DIAMOND

Crack-lin' Ros-ie, get on board. We're gon-na ride till there ain't no more to go, tak-in' it slow. And Lord don't you know I'll

PLAY ME

Words and Music by
NEIL DIAMOND

You are the sun, I am the moon, you are the words, I am the tune: play ___ me. ___

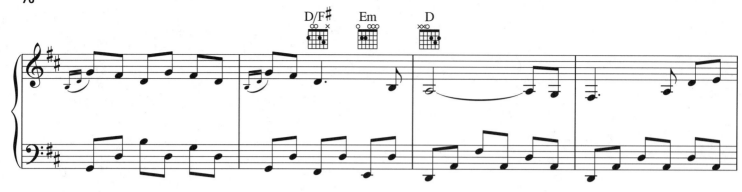

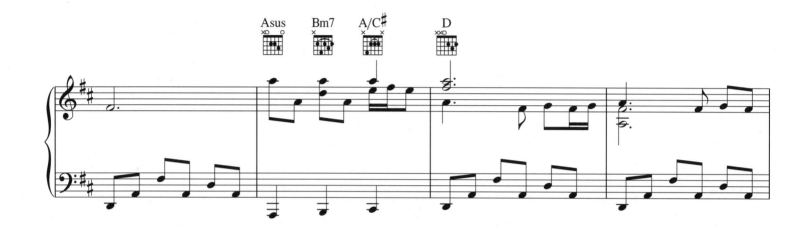

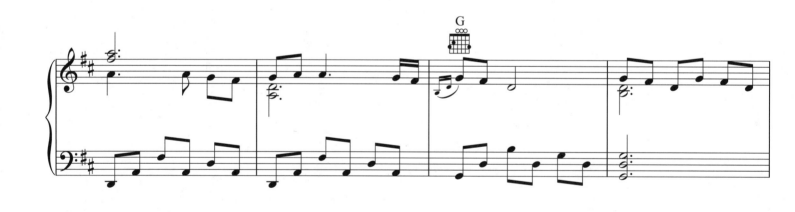

D.S. al Coda

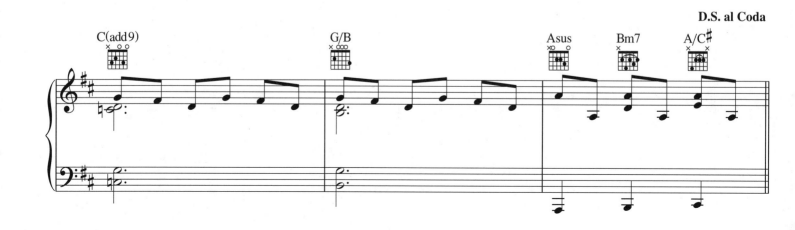

MORNINGSIDE
(For My Children)

Words and Music by
NEIL DIAMOND

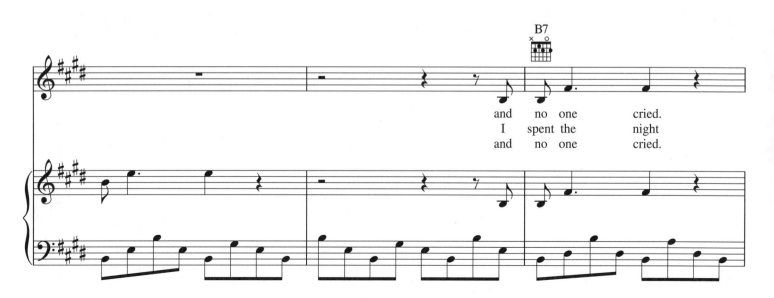

CRUNCHY GRANOLA SUITE

Words and Music by
NEIL DIAMOND

Da __ da da da   da __ da da

Let me hear___ that, get___ ___me near___ that Crunch-y Gran-o-la Suite.___

Drop your shrink __ and stop __ your drink - in'; crunch-y gran-o-la's neat! __

Sing it out, ____ all

right.

BROOKLYN ROADS

Words and Music by
NEIL DIAMOND

D.S. al Coda

CODA

Brook - lyn   roads. __

SOOLAIMON

Words and Music by
NEIL DIAMOND

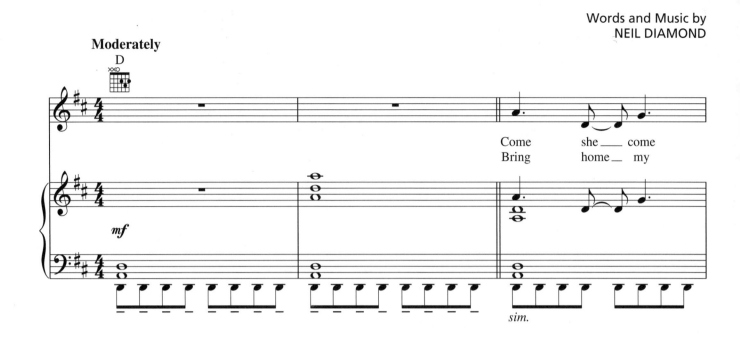

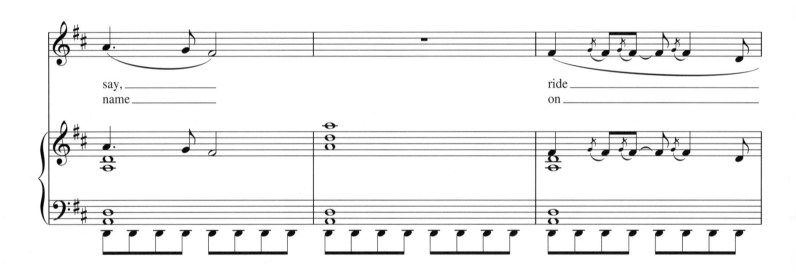

AMERICA
from the Motion Picture THE JAZZ SINGER

Words and Music by
NEIL DIAMOND

Free, on - ly want to be free.

We hud - dle close, hang on to a dream.

On the boats and on the planes, they're com - ing to A - mer - i - ca.

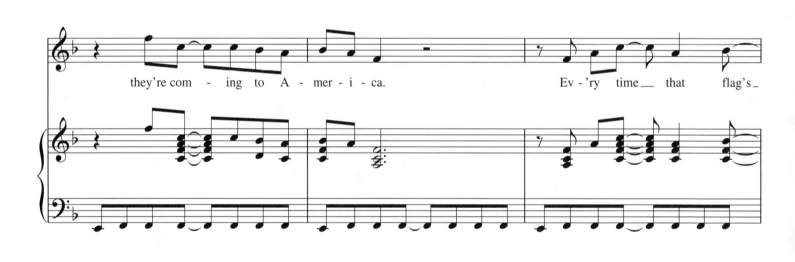

Ev -'ry-where a - round___ the world,

they're com - ing to A - mer - i - ca.

Ev -'ry time___ that flag's_

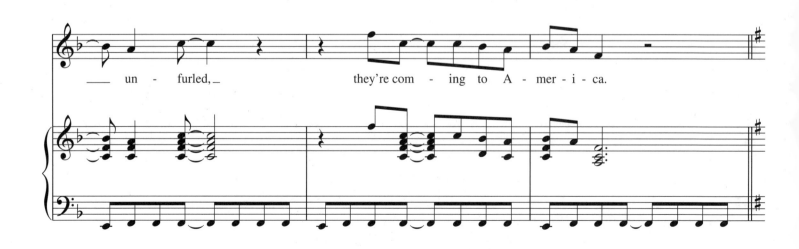

___ un - furled,_

they're com - ing to A - mer - i - ca.

My coun-try 'tis of thee (to-day),___ sweet_ land of
lib-er-ty (to-day),___ of thee I sing___ (to-day),___
___ of thee I sing___ to-day.___

Repeat and Fade

To-day,___ to-day.___

HELLO AGAIN

from the Motion Picture THE JAZZ SINGER

Words by NEIL DIAMOND
Music by NEIL DIAMOND and ALAN LINDGREN

LOVE ON THE ROCKS
from the Motion Picture THE JAZZ SINGER

Words and Music by NEIL DIAMOND
and GILBERT BECAUD

Love on the rocks

ain't no sur-prise.

Pour me a drink, __ and I'll

tell you some lies. __

Got noth-in' to lose, __ so you

To Coda

CAPTAIN SUNSHINE

Words and Music by
NEIL DIAMOND

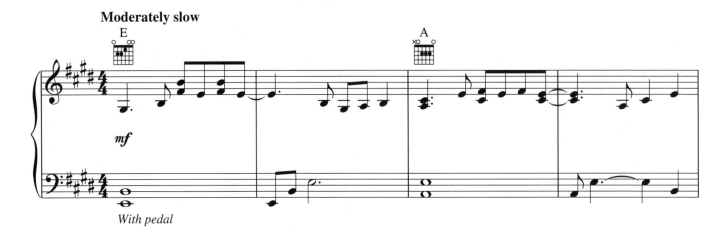

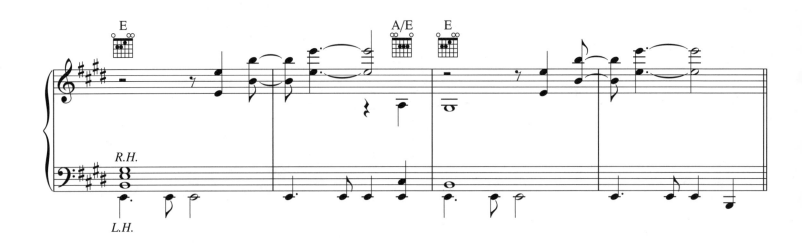

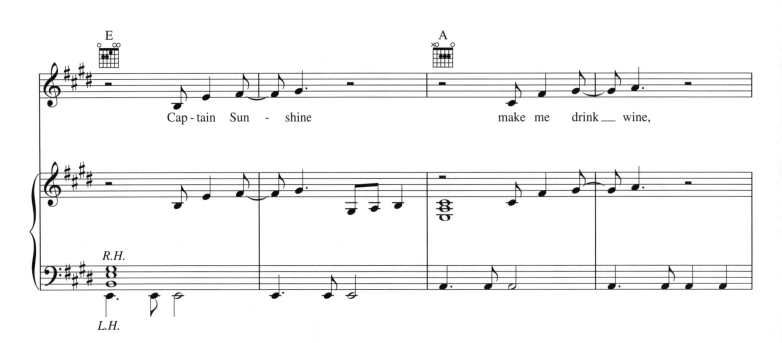

Cap - tain Sun - shine   make me drink __ wine,

tween the earth_ and the sea._

He _____ don't_ take much. _____ He _____ don't make_ much.

HE AIN'T HEAVY...
HE'S MY BROTHER

Words and Music by BOB RUSSELL
and BOBBY SCOTT

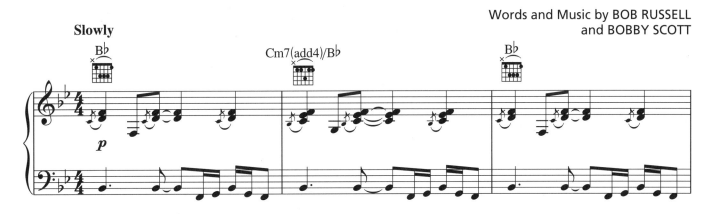

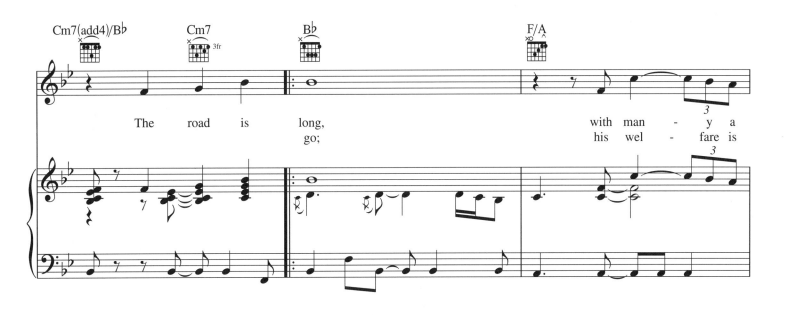

The road is long,
go;
with man - y a
his wel - fare is

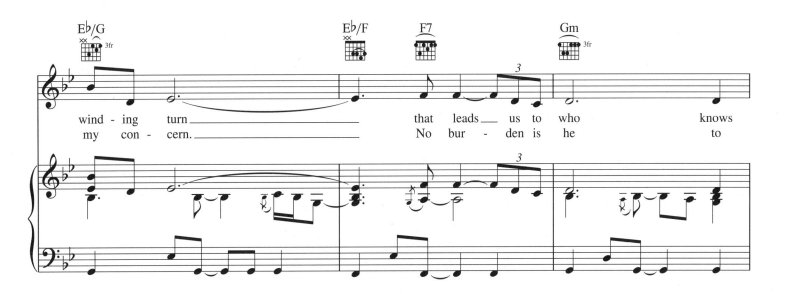

wind - ing turn _____ that leads ___ us to who knows
my con - cern. _____ No bur - den is he to

YES I WILL

Words and Music by
NEIL DIAMOND

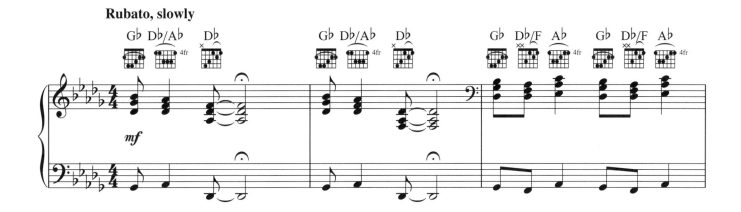

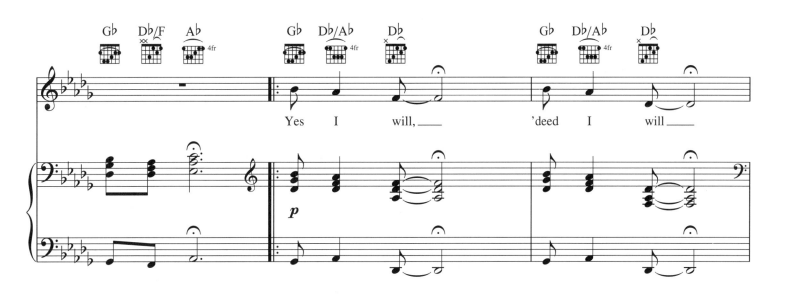

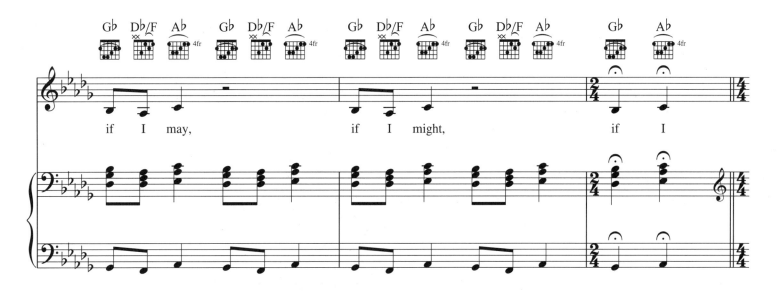

say it out loud if you need to be ho - ly; so you do, so you want to be lov - ing,

say it out now if you need to be ho - li - er still.

ff

decresc.

D.S. al Coda

LADY MAGDELENE

Words and Music by
NEIL DIAMOND

The man on the right ___ is a man un-done. ___
The man on the left ___ is a prize un-won, ___
The man in be-tween ___ waits be-tween the two, ___

that love is a song____ for
the man on the left,____ the
and there he will sleep,____ the

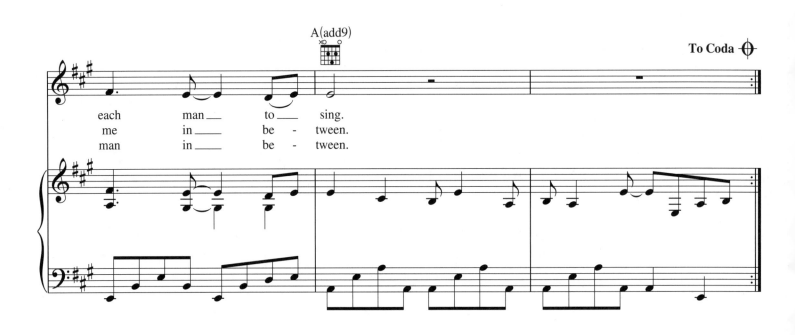

each man ____ to ____ sing.
me in ____ be - tween.
man in ____ be - tween.

To Coda ⊕

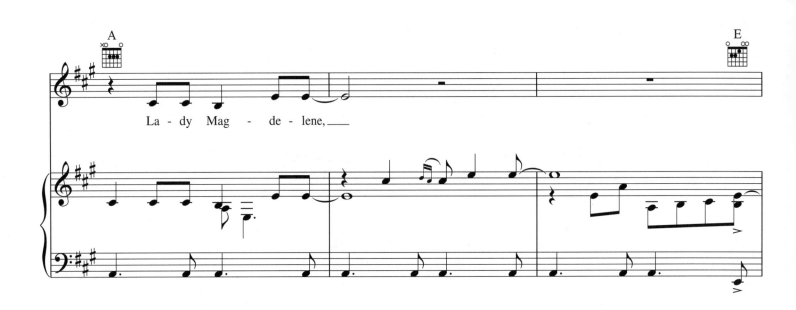

La - dy Mag - de - lene,____

where we are.＿

Take us to your soul＿

＿ for we have wan - dered far.＿

SHILO

Words and Music by
NEIL DIAMOND

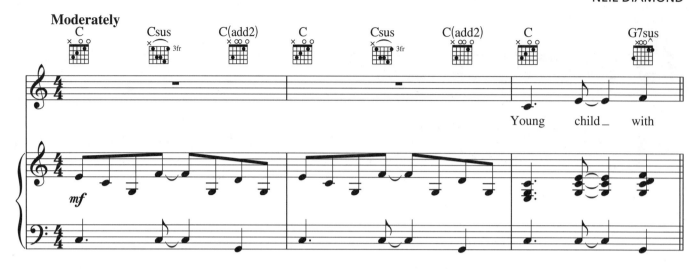

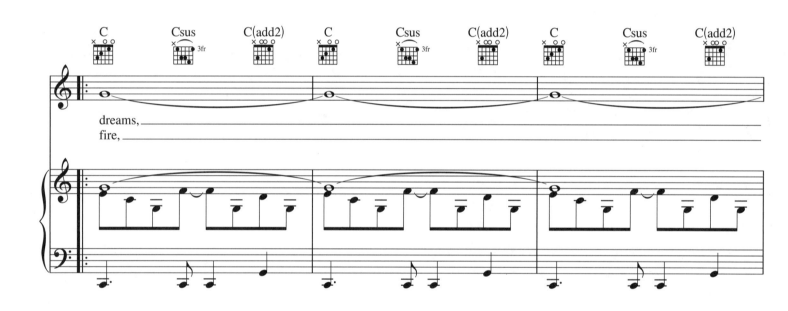

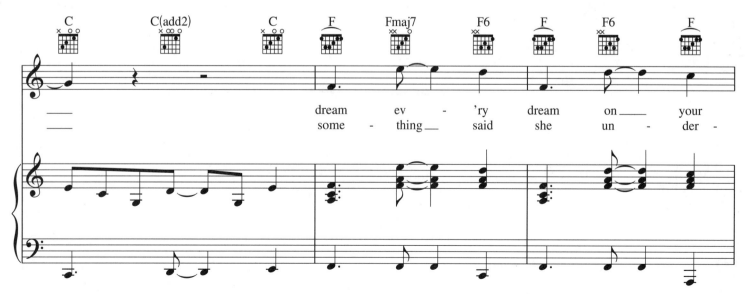

BROTHER LOVE'S TRAVELING SALVATION SHOW

Words and Music by
NEIL DIAMOND

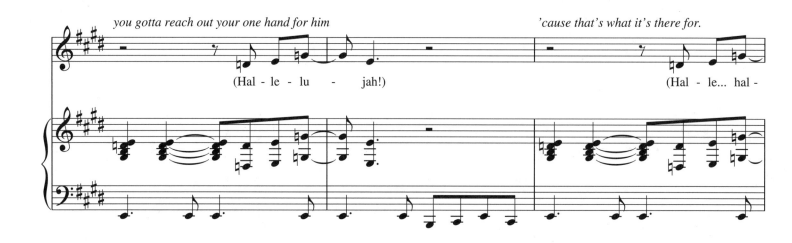

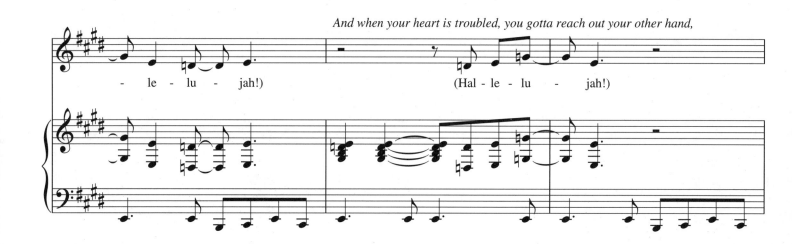

IF YOU KNOW WHAT I MEAN

Words and Music by
NEIL DIAMOND

When the night re - turns just like a friend,

when the eve - ning comes to set me free, ___ when the qui - et hours that wait be -

yond the day make peace - ful sounds in me. ___

BEAUTIFUL NOISE

Words and Music by
NEIL DIAMOND

YOU DON'T BRING ME FLOWERS

Words by NEIL DIAMOND,
MARILYN BERGMAN and ALAN BERGMAN
Music by NEIL DIAMOND

Slowly and freely

You don't bring me flow - ers; you don't sing me love songs.

You hard - ly talk to me an - y - more when you come through the door at the end of the day.

I re - mem - ber when you could - n't wait to love me,

DESIRÉE

Words and Music by
NEIL DIAMOND

FOREVER IN BLUE JEANS

Words and Music by NEIL DIAMOND
and RICHARD BENNETT

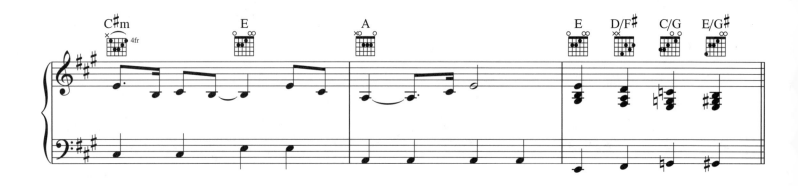

Mon-ey talks.___ But it don't sing and dance,___ and it don't walk.___

SEPTEMBER MORN

Words and Music by NEIL DIAMOND
and GILBERT BECAUD

Moderately slow

Stay for just a while. Stay and let me look at you.

It's been so long, I hard-ly knew you stand-ing in the door.

Stay with me a while. I on-ly wan-na talk to you.

I'VE BEEN THIS WAY BEFORE

Words and Music by
NEIL DIAMOND

YESTERDAY'S SONGS

Words and Music by
NEIL DIAMOND

(Say-in' I love __ you, now, ba-by, say-in' I love __ you, now,

ba - by.)

Yes - ter - day's songs __ don't
Yes - ter - day's songs __ don't

stay a - round __ long, __ not much an - y - more. __
seem to be - long. __ They're here and they're gone. __

HEARTLIGHT

Words and Music by NEIL DIAMOND,
BURT BACHARACH and CAROLE BAYER SAGER

Light Rock Ballad

And home is the most ex - cel - lent place of all. _____ And I'll be right here if

HEADED FOR THE FUTURE

Words by NEIL DIAMOND
Music by NEIL DIAMOND, TOM HENSLEY
and ALAN LINDGREN

now.

Show you _____ how. _____

YOU ARE THE BEST PART OF ME

Words and Music by
NEIL DIAMOND